At the
airport

INTRODUCTION

An airport – especially a busy international one, such as Heathrow – is a very exciting place. People of all nationalities are continuously travelling to and from many different countries around the world. In fact, millions of passengers may pass through an airport every year.

Just imagine how complicated it must be to manage an airport. People need to get there, so airports need car parks, bus stops, taxi ranks, and railway stations. When you arrive, you will have to check in with your chosen airline and your baggage must be handled as well as checked to make sure you are carrying nothing dangerous or illegal. There are places to eat and drink, toilets, showers, places to change a baby, and places to worship. There are shops where you can buy all kinds of things from books, magazines and sweets to souvenirs or even clothes. You must be able to find out where to go and what to do so there are information desks and a variety of signs.

You must then pass through immigration, where your passport is checked, then on to a further security check before entering the main departure lounge. You will have your hand luggage X-rayed or searched and you may be searched yourself. In the main departure lounge there are more places to eat, drink and shop. Information boards tell you what time your flight is due to depart and from which gate. You may need to use a moving walkway or cross a skybridge. Finally, you will board your plane either via a jetty or airbridge, or even by walking across the tarmac (apron), and up the steps.

When you travel, it can be an exciting experience – there is so much to see around you. You can get even more out of every flight and visit to the airport if you take i-SPY At the Airport with you when you travel.

How to use your I-SPY book

As you work through this book, you will notice that the subjects are arranged in groups which are related to the kinds of places where you are likely to find things. You need 1000 points to send off for your i-SPY certificate (see page 64) but that is not too difficult because there are masses of points in every book. Each entry has a star or circle and points value beside it. The stars represent harder to spot entries. As you make each i-SPY, write your score in the circle or star.

Airports are usually located where there is enough flat land to allow for one or more level runways to be built as well as the other buildings and structures needed. When new airports are built, the designers also try to keep disturbances to local people to a minimum. Finally, the natural environment must be taken into account. All this means that airports may be some distance from towns or cities and anyone wishing to travel by air must first be able to get to the airport. There are various ways to approach most airports.

Points: 5

TAXI

Taxis are one of the most popular ways of getting to and from airports, due to the fact that travellers often have luggage, are often on tight schedules and don't want to leave their cars for long periods in car parks.

TRAIN

Points: 10

You may have travelled to the airport by rapid transport system like the London Underground (tube) or the Tyne and Wear Metro, or you may have travelled by overland train. Many airports have a dedicated train or tube service that takes you to and from the local city centre.

If you travel by car, it is most likely that you will have parked in one of the long-term car parks.

PARKING ZONE

Points: 10

Remember where you leave your car! Most car parks are very large and it is important to make a note of your parking place.

Points: 5

BUS STOP

You can catch the courtesy bus to the airport terminal from one of the bus stops. Make a note of this stop as it will be the one you need to return to when you collect the car.

PARKING PAYMENT

Points: 5

Automatic payment machines are located at the car park and often in the airport terminal as well.

Points: 10

EXPRESS COACH

Express coaches operate between the airport and several other urban centres.

TRANSFER BUS

Points: 5

At a big airport, where there are several terminals, you may need to catch a bus from the long-term car park, or between terminals.

An airport terminal may offer all kinds of facilities. These can be especially useful if you have forgotten something or if you have a long time to wait at an airport.

PORTER

Points: 25

Whether you arrive by bus, taxi, train or car, you may be able to find a smartly-uniformed porter who will, for a fee, take your luggage to the check-in desk, although these are becoming a very rare sight at UK airports.

 Points: 15

VALET PARKING

Drive to the airport and this service parks your car for you, at a destination away from the airport. When you return from your trip, it will be waiting outside the airport terminal!

BAGGAGE TROLLEY

Points: 5

You can always use a baggage trolley yourself. Look for these at a trolley park around the terminal building.

Points: 5

INFORMATION DESK

Whether you are a passenger or not, you may need to find out if a flight has arrived or where you can hire a car. Whatever information you need, the staff at an information desk will try to help.

TELEPHONE

Points: 10

Calling overseas is an easy task on the phone systems in most airports.

Points: 10

CHARITY AND DONATIONS

You will find some discreetly positioned charity boxes. All the proceeds given go to very good causes and coins (and notes!) of any currency are usually accepted – a great way to make good use of your leftover foreign currency!

PHOTO BOOTH

Points: 10

By the time you reach the airport, it's too late to be getting a passport photograph. On the other hand, these booths do provide quick and easy photographs.

Points: 15

POST OFFICE

You can even find a post office at the airport – important for buying stamps for that last-minute letter or postcard. Post them in the postbox that you may find at the post office or around the terminal building.

BUREAU DE CHANGE

Points: 5

At a bureau de change you can change money from one currency to another, such as UK pounds into US dollars or euros.

SHOPS

Michaelpuche / Shutterstock.com

Many airports have a collection of shops. The range of shops can vary dramatically depending on how big or how busy the airport is. Some shops are for the travellers' convenience selling food and drink, confectionery, newspapers and magazines. Others stock items popular with people going on trips like books, adapter plugs and toiletries. Most airports will usually have shops selling more expensive items and gifts like designer clothing, jewelry and watches. Some of the shops are tax free! Score for spotting any of these items:

 Points: 10

A bottle of perfume or aftershave

 Points: 20

A designer shirt or dress

 Points: 15

A novel from the 'top ten'

 Points: 30 Top Spot!

A piece of diamond jewellery

ATM

Points: 5

Cash machines are always available when you need money.

Points: 5

TV MONITOR

You can catch up with world news and events on large TV displays situated in airport lounges.

GAMES CENTRE

Points: 15

It is now possible to play some of your favourite electronic games when waiting at an airport.

Points: 10

DRINKING FOUNTAIN

If you're thirsty find a drinking fountain in the airport for a drink of water.

Points: 5

RESTAURANT

You might need a snack, or a main meal. There are usually a variety of bars, cafes and restaurants at most airports.

INTERNET

Points: 10

It's quite easy to keep in touch by e-mail or surf the web at one of these special internet stations. Alternatively you may find the airport has areas of Wi-Fi.

Points: 25 Top Spot!

KIDS' ZONE

Young children can easily get bored waiting at an airport. This specially-designed children's lounge is the perfect way to keep them occupied.

SECURITY DOG

Top Spot!   Points: 30

You won't find one of these sniffer dogs at every airport but they are highly trained to search and find illegal substances.

Points: 10

TERMINAL INDICATOR

Large airports have several terminals and signs like these will help direct you to the correct terminal for your flight.

TRAVELATOR

Points: 10

You may need to travel within the terminal by moving walkway. This looks like a flat escalator and can save you walking long distances within the terminal.

Points: 15

COVERED WALKWAY

Have a look where you are walking. If you have to leave one building and travel to another, you may walk along an enclosed bridge (called a skybridge) connecting the two.

INFORMATION BOARD

Points: 15

These digital displays are really useful for providing up-to-date information about flights. You need to check the board to see if your flight is on time, where to check in and which gate your flight will be departing from. Some boards will list arriving flights if you are meeting someone at the airport.

Points: 10

SHUTTLE TRAIN

To reach your checking-in point you may need to travel on an internal shuttle system between terminals. There are may shuttle types from a monorail train (e.g. a sky train) to an underground tube.

CONCOURSE

Points: 15

A concourse is a large public open space and modern terminal buildings can have some impressive architecture to surround this space. This picture shows Heathrow's Terminal 5 – the largest freestanding structure in the UK.

Points: 20

PRAYER ROOM

Airports are not just about rushing around and catching a flight. You can find these special prayer rooms if you need time to reflect and say some prayers.

If you are going to travel by air, one of the first things that you will have to do when you arrive at the airport is check in with the airline that you are travelling with. For most international flights you should check in around two hours before your flight is due to depart. You will need to show your ticket and passport, your luggage will be weighed and checked in and you will be issued with a boarding card. You will also be asked questions about the security of your luggage. For some flights you can check in online before you travel and then drop your bag at the 'bag drop' area when you arrive at the terminal.

TRAVEL RESTRICTIONS

Points: 5

You will find signs like this in several places around the check-in area. They tell you what you are not allowed to take on board the aircraft and must be obeyed.

Points: 10 **LIQUIDS**

Only containers of under 100ml are currently allowed in hand luggage and these all need to be in a small, clear plastic bag when you go through security checks.

HAND LUGGAGE

Points: 10

There is limited space on an aeroplane and you cannot take large bags or packages in the cabin. If your bag can fit into a container like this one, you may take it on with you. Be careful, as different airline companies have different size restrictions.

Points: 10

CHECK-IN DESK

If you use the check-in desk, you will be asked a number of security questions, your luggage will be weighed and identification tags put on them. This makes sure that your bags arrive at the same airport as you do, on the same flight!

FIRST CLASS

Points: 15

If you are lucky enough to be travelling first or business class, you will have your own separate check-in facilities. Some airports also have a fast track system to allow these passengers to board more quickly.

SELF-SERVICE

Points: 10

You can save time by having your tickets issued on the internet and by checking in on the self-service machines. There are always plenty of staff available to help if you need assistance. Not all airlines will have them but here are a selection of check-in machines.

OVERSIZED LUGGAGE

Points: 20

Some people have to travel with very large packages or bulky items like skis or pushchairs. If this is the case, they will be taken to a special oversized luggage area to be checked in. There may be an excess baggage fee to pay.

Points: 10

PASSPORT CONTROL

When you are ready and have finished checking in, you will need to make your way to passport control.

Security is essential at all airports and you will be required to have your possessions examined and X-rayed. Often you will be asked to stand with your arms out, so your body can be searched.

Points: 15

Some airports can now check your passport by electronically scanning the details.

Points: 25 **Top Spot!**

IRIS RECOGNITION

As everyone's eyes are different, iris recognition is used as part of the security check at some airports. Your iris is scanned, and as long as it matches with the image on record your identity can be confirmed. This scan may be done at check in and when you go through immigration at your destination.

Points: 10

You will need to put any metal objects, including keys, mobile telephones, money and even belt buckles and shoes into a plastic tray that is checked though an X-ray machine.

Points: 15

The X-ray scanner allows bags to be viewed to check their contents. Each item has to be scanned and checked to make sure that it is safe to be allowed on the aeroplane. The operators of the machines are skilled technicians who know exactly what to look for when they see the images. If they see anything suspicious, the item will be removed and checked by hand.

Points: 20

HAND-HELD WAND

To be certain that you are carrying nothing illegal, and to reinforce the previous searches, you may see a hand-held wand in use. This device is a portable metal detector that can be passed all over the body to be certain that you are not carrying anything illegal.

X-RAY IMAGES

Points: 20

By picking up metal objects as a solid image, any headphones, electronic components, clasps, buckles etc. will show up. Anything that is considered dangerous, such as knives, scissors or even knitting needles can be confiscated.

Points: 10

WALK-THROUGH METAL DETECTOR

This is another type of X-ray machine. As you walk through the frame, an alarm is immediately activated if it senses any metal. This could be a belt buckle, keys in a pocket or a watch. You will be asked to remove these items and go through the scanner again.

Points: 15

BODY SEARCH

Regardless of the results of the walk-through detector, you may also be given a body search. Here a member of security will check your clothes to make sure that nothing is being smuggled on board.

DEPARTURE GATE SIGN

Points: 10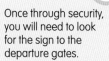

Once through security, you will need to look for the sign to the departure gates.

 Points: 10

DEPARTURE GATES

You will need to find the departure gate for your flight in good time before boarding. In many larger airports there are numerous gates so getting to the right one could mean a long walk or even a journey on an internal shuttle train.

24

Points: 5

DEPARTURE BOARD

One last check on the departure board to make sure the flight is on time.

LOUNGE

Points: 15

You may be lucky enough to be allowed to check in to a private lounge. These are normally only for people travelling first and business class, or by private plane.

Points: 15

TRANSIT BUS

Aircraft have to park at their designated parking space. This may be some way from the departure gate. Often a transit bus will take you safely and quickly from the departure gate to the aircraft steps.

At some airports, you may either have to walk across the apron (tarmac) to board the aircraft or you will be taken in a transit bus. As you go, keep a look out on the tarmac: there are all kinds of interesting things to see.

JETTIES

Here is one of the jetties or airbridges that allow passengers to walk straight through from the departure lounge to the door of the aircraft…

 Points: 10

…and here is a jetty being joined to an aircraft.

 Points: 15

Steps were once the most common way to board an aircraft and are still used to board many aircraft, particularly at smaller airports.

STEPS

Points: 10

Points: 15

Enclosed steps like those above, make sure that you do not get wet when it is raining!

The steps in the picture above are the most common and you will find these being used to board many aircraft.

Smaller planes do not need large steps and you may see trucks with steps like these in the picture on the right. These are easy to move and can be quickly manoeuvred into position.

Points: 20

When you have a meal or a drink on an aeroplane, have you ever stopped to think how the food arrived on board? A catering truck pulls up alongside and when in position, the container is raised by hydraulic lifts until it is level with the opening hatch. The carefully packed food and drink can then be slid along tracks into the hold compartment of the plane.

FREIGHT

Points: 15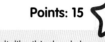

A conveyor belt, like this, loads bags and parcels on to an aircraft. It is usually known as a rocket.

 Points: 15

PASSENGERS' BAGGAGE

Passengers' baggage is usually carried to the aircraft in containers on wheeled trollies, called dollies. The containers are known as bins.

HI-LOADER

Points: 15

Here is another type of freight vehicle – this one is known as a hi-loader.

 Points: 15

TUG

Sometimes, aircraft must be moved in or out of their parking positions by special, powerful vehicles, called tugs.

29

BAGGAGE HANDLING

Points: 5

All the suitcases and bags have to be loaded on to the correct aircraft to make sure that they arrive with you at your destination.

Points: 20

HIGH RISER

This platform allows access to the passenger deck so meals and toiletries can be replenished.

SECURED CONTAINERS

Points: 20

It is important that the contents of any goods that are being loaded are secure and do not fall over or collapse when being moved. Most palletised loads are strapped and secured for loading.

Points: 35   Top Spot!   **LARGE LOADS**

Sometimes aircraft have to carry really large loads. Some cargo aircraft are specially designed to be able to carry these consignments – if you are lucky you may see one being loaded. Look how the nose section opens up completely.

All aircraft need fuel. The aviation fuel is generally taken to the plane so that it can be refuelled on the apron. Here are some examples.

POWER TRACK

Points: 20

When an aircraft is on its parking stand, ground power is supplied along one of these power tracks.

 Points: 10

FUEL TRUCK

You may see a fuel truck under the wing of an aeroplane with pipes connecting it directly to the fuel tanks. Score 10 points if you can see the fuel truck standing by or in transit to an aircraft.

REFUELLING

Points: 20

Many larger passenger aircraft store some of the fuel in their wings. Score 20 points if you can actually see the fuel pipe being connected to an aircraft.

Points: 30   **Top Spot!**

HELICOPTER

You would expect to see aeroplanes at most international airports, but helicopters also fly from many domestic and local ones. Helicopters tend to be used on short flights within the same country. They are popular for sightseeing flights around major landmarks. Most helicopters have a single rotor, but some larger freight-carrying helicopters and many military helicopters have two rotors.

Points: 20

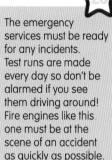

The emergency services must be ready for any incidents. Test runs are made every day so don't be alarmed if you see them driving around! Fire engines like this one must be at the scene of an accident as quickly as possible.

Points: 20

AMBULANCE

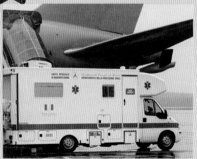

An airport is a very busy place with thousands of people travelling through it every day. Airports can have their own ambulance services which offer assistance to people who fall ill at the airport, as well dealing with any accidents that may occur from time to time.

34

Here are a few signs that you may see from the aircraft window, or outside the terminal building.

Points: 20

STOP AND LOOK

The many vehicles that work in and around the airport all have to comply with strict traffic controls. This sign indicates that aircraft always have the right of way!

AIRCRAFT VIEWING AREA

Points: 15

Watching or spotting aircraft is a hobby that many people enjoy. Some airports have designated viewing areas, often on the roof or a balcony where you can watch and take pictures of planes landing and taking off.

Points: 30 Top Spot!

EMERGENCY SERVICES

In the event of a major incident, it is vital that the emergency services take control of the situation as quickly as possible. You may see an emergency services rendevous point sign like this one.

SECURITY FENCE

Points: 15

Airports must be secure places and it is vital that no one can enter the airport complex unless they have the correct security clearances and permissions. A tall perimeter fence will encircle most airports.

Points: 10

WINDSOCK

These colourful material tubes are secured to the top of a post at most airports to indicate the wind direction.

RUNWAY AHEAD

Points: 20

You are most likely to see this sign from the aeroplane window just before you take off!

SECURITY CAMERAS

Security cameras are prominent on both the terminal building and on the runway. This one is watching the area close to the terminal...

...and this one is near the runway out in the middle of the airfield.

LANDING LIGHTS

Airfields are well lit at night, with lights on both the sides of the runway, as well as approach markers indicating the beginning of the runway.

CONTROL TOWER

Points: 5

All flight movements are controlled from the air traffic control tower. The control tower is usually the tallest building at an airport.

Points: 10

RADAR

A radar system is used to confirm the position of aircraft near the airport. From the radar screen the operator can give instructions to pilots who are taking off, landing and taxiing.

HANGAR

Points: 15

When an aircraft needs maintenance it will be taken to a large hangar. These structures are normally located away from the terminal building.

CHOCKS

Points: 15

A chock is a sturdy piece of material, placed behind a wheel to prevent accidental movement when the aircraft is parked.

Points: 10

SETS OF WHEELS

A large aeroplane will have many wheels. The tyres on these wheels have to be incredibly strong to withstand the force of landing.

COCKPIT

Top Spot!   Points: 30

If you are lucky enough, you may see the pilots in the cockpit.

MOVING AROUND

Points: 15

Ground staff use hand signals to assist the pilot in parking the aeroplane at the correct gate.

Points: 10

TAKE OFF

One of the many sights that you will see at an airport is an aeroplane taking off. You will probably be able to see these from the terminal windows.

ARRIVALS

Points: 5

When you arrive at your destination, you will need to follow signs for 'arrivals'. This will take you to the right area for customs clearance and to find your bags and suitcases.

 Points: 10

BAGGAGE RECLAIM

Wherever you have travelled from, you will need to collect your bags before you leave the airport. Look for signs like this one for baggage reclaim to retrieve your bags.

BAGGAGE CAROUSEL

Points: 10

When you reach the arrivals hall, check the notice board to see which baggage carousel your bags will be on. All the bags and suitcases from that flight will be going around, so be sure to double-check the bags you take really are yours!

Not all journeys end when the aeroplane touches down on the runway. You may need to catch another flight to reach your destination. If so, you may need to follow a sign like this one…

 Points: 10

…or one like this, without words.

 Points: 15

When you have cleared immigration and collected your bags you will need to pass through customs. The passage you take (colour coded in UK airports) will depend on where you have travelled from and what you are carrying.

Points: 15

GREEN CHANNEL

You can go through the green channel if you are travelling from a country outside the European Union, if you are carrying no more than the regular customs allowance and if you are carrying no banned or restricted goods.

BLUE CHANNEL

Points: 15

Go through the blue channel if you are travelling from a country within the European Union and you have no banned or restricted goods.

Points: 15

RED CHANNEL

The red channel should be used if you have goods to declare, have commercial goods or if you are not sure which channel to go through.

UK BORDER

Points: 15

If you are travelling from overseas, you will need to have your passport checked to formally enter the United Kingdom. The immigration officer will do this when your passport is checked at the desk.

 Points: 20

PERSON WITH SIGN

Some people, especially those travelling on business, are collected at the airport, normally by a driver with a car. You will see the driver holding up a sign with the customer's name, or company name on it.

TOURIST INFORMATION

Points: 10

Once you are through customs, you may find an information display. This may contain leaflets with maps and details of local places to visit or it may be a digital touch-screen terminal.

Points: 20

RESTRICTED ZONE

Many areas within the airport are not open to the general public and you are not allowed to enter them. These places are known as restricted zones or areas.

SECURITY KEYPAD

Points: 15

Keypads allow airport staff to pass through secured and locked doors with a special number sequence.

Points: 15

INFORMATION SIGN

Look out for signs like this one that tell you what you are not allowed to do in certain areas of the airport. Can you spot any others?

ADRIA AIRWAYS

Points: 20

AER LINGUS

Points: 5

AEROFLOT

Points: 20

AIR ALGÉRIE

Points: 25

AIR CANADA

Points: 15

AIR FRANCE

Points: 10

Points: 35   **Top Spot!**   **AIR SEYCHELLES**

EGley / Shutterstock.com

Air Seychelles was established in the late 1970s. The airline offers regular flights between the islands of the Seychelles but also further afield to major cities predominantly in Africa such as Durban, Johannesburg and Antananarivo, as well as to the other Indian Ocean nations like Mauritius. In 2013 Air Seychelles began regular flights into Europe although their planes are not easy to spot on the tarmac in the UK especially at airports outside of London.

AIR INDIA

 Points: 15

AIR MALTA

 Points: 15

AIR NEW ZEALAND

 Points: 25

AIR SLOVAKIA

 Points: 20

ALITALIA

 Points: 10

AMERICAN AIRLINES

 Points: 5

AUSTRIAN AIRLINES ⭐20 Points: 20

Chris Parypa Photography / Shutterstock.com

AVIANCA Top Spot! Points: 30 ⭐30

Tupungato / Shutterstock.com

BH AIR ⭐15 Points: 15

BMI REGIONAL

VanderWolf Images / Shutterstock.com

10 Points: 10

BRITISH AIRWAYS

ByChrisVanLennepPhoto / Shutterstock.com

5 Points: 5

BULGARIA AIR

Senohrabek / Shutterstock.com

20 Points: 20

CARIBBEAN AIRLINES

Chris Parypa Photography / Shutterstock.com

25 Points: 25

CATHAY PACIFIC

byeolson / Shutterstock.com

10 Points: 10

CHINA AIRLINES

Sorbis / Shutterstock.com

15 Points: 15

CHINA EASTERN AIRLINES · Points: 25

nfinut380 / Shutterstock.com

CHINA SOUTHERN AIRLINES · Top Spot! · Points: 30

Chameleonseye / Shutterstock.com

CROATIA AIRLINES · Points: 20

Markus Mainka / Shutterstock.com

DELTA

Points: 10

DHL

Points: 15

EASYJET

Points: 5

EL AL

Points: 15

EMIRATES

Points: 5

ETIHAD AIRWAYS

Points: 10

EGYPTAIR   20   Points: 20

Philip Lange / Shutterstock.com

ETHIOPIAN AIRLINES   25   Points: 25

Vytautas Kielaitis / Shutterstock.com

HELVETIC AIRWAYS   20   Points: 20

Vytautas Kielaitis / Shutterstock.com

35

Points: 35   Top Spot!   EVA AIR

Mike Fuchslocher / Shutterstock.com

EVA Air (or more correctly E V A Air – with the letters pronounced) is one of the largest airline operators based in Taiwan. They fly passengers and cargo mainly on routes in and around eastern Asia, with their base being Taipei, Taiwan. EVA Air flies to several European destinations via Bangkok. They are a relatively young airline being founded in 1989 and as such they have a modern fleet and an excellent safety record.

FEDEX

Points: 15

FINNAIR

Points: 15

FLYBE

Points: 10

IBERIA

Points: 10

JAPAN AIRLINES

Points: 15

KLM

Points: 10

ICELANDAIR — Points: 15

Vytautas Kielaitis / Shutterstock.com

IRAN AIR — Points: 25

Markus Mainka / Shutterstock.com

LOT POLISH AIRLINES — Points: 20

Przemyslaw Szablowski / Shutterstock.com

KOREAN AIR

Top Spot! Points: 30

Chris Parypa Photography / Shutterstock.com

KUWAIT AIRLINES

Points: 25

Markus / Monika / Shutterstock.com

LUFTHANSA

Points: 10

Karasev Victor / Shutterstock.com

MALAYSIA AIRLINES

Foz Zaki / Shutterstock.com

Points: 20

MIDDLE EAST AIRLINES

Rébius / Shutterstock.com

Points: 15

MONARCH

Craig Russell / Shutterstock.com

Points: 10

NORWEGIAN

Craig Russell / Shutterstock.com

Points: 10

OLYMPIC AIR

Robert Szrosiak / Shutterstock.com

Points: 15

PAKISTAN INTERNATIONAL

Mehdi Photos / Shutterstock.com

Points: 25

QANTAS

Mike Fuchslocher / Shutterstock.com

Points: 10

QATAR AIRWAYS

Craig Russell / Shutterstock.com

Points: 10

ROYAL JORDANIAN

turbo83 / Shutterstock.com

Points: 20

RYANAIR

EI-EVM

Craig Russell / Shutterstock.com

Points: 5

SAS

VanderWolf Images / Shutterstock.com

Points: 10

SINGAPORE AIRLINES

Dmitry Birin / Shutterstock.com

Points: 10

Points: 40 Top Spot!

ROYAL BRUNEI AIRLINES

Larro Lani / Shutterstock.com

Headquartered in Bandar Seri Begawan the capital of Brunei this airline is the national flag carrier of that country. Royal Brunei flies to destinations predominantly around Australia and south-east Asia but also offers long-haul flights to the UK via Dubai.

SOUTH AFRICAN AIRWAYS

Tupungato / Shutterstock.com

Points: 10

SRI LANKAN AIRLINES

Davide Calabresi / Shutterstock.com

Points: 25

SWISS

Arseny Krasnevsky / Shutterstock.com

Points: 10

TAP PORTUGAL

Craig Russell / Shutterstock.com

Points: 15

THAI AIRWAYS

VanderWolf Images / Shutterstock.com

Points: 15

THOMAS COOK

Markus Mainka / Shutterstock.com

Points: 5

THOMSON

Nukkamol Komolwanich / Shutterstock.com

5 Points: 5

TURKISH AIRLINES

InsectWorld / Shutterstock.com

20 Points: 20

UNITED AIRLINES

InsectWorld / Shutterstock.com

10 Points: 10

VIRGIN ATLANTIC

Chris Parypa Photography / Shutterstock.com

5 Points: 5

VUELING

Markus Mainka / Shutterstock.com

15 Points: 15

WIZZ AIR

InsectWorld / Shutterstock.com

10 Points: 10

i-SPY

How to get your
i-SPY certificate
and badge

Let us know when you've become
a super-spotter with 1000 points
and we'll send you a special
certificate and badge!

HERE'S
WHAT
TO DO!

- ✓ Ask an adult to check your score.

- ✓ Visit www.collins.co.uk/i-SPY to
  apply for your certificate. If you
  are under the age of 13 you will need
  a parent or guardian to do this.

- ✓ We'll send your certificate via
  email and you'll receive a brilliant
  badge through the post!